Learning Words

Colin Clark

Illustrated by Lesley McLaren

Published by Peter Haddock Ltd
Bridlington, England
© Peter Haddock Ltd
Printed and bound in the United Kingdom

Learning Words

words about you, me and us

When we know someone's **age**, we know the number of years he or she has lived.

Your **arm** is the part between your shoulder and your hand. We have two **arms**.

The elbow is the joint between your upper **arm** and your lower **arm**, or fore**arm**.

An **aunt** is either your mother's sister, or your father's sister, or your uncle's wife.

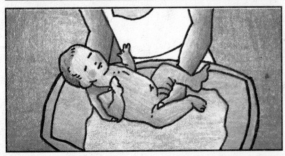

A **baby** is a very young child. The youngest member of a family is the **baby**.

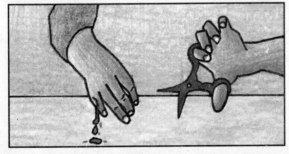

Blood is the red liquid inside our bodies. If we cut a finger, **blood** flows out.

The **body** is everything solid in a person or an animal. Our **bodies** are covered by skin.

The **body** can also be the main part of a person, an animal, a plant, or a thing, not including the head, the arms, the legs, the wings or tail.

We all have **bones** inside our bodies. **Bones** are hard, and they support the body.

All our **bones** together make up a frame inside us. The frame is called a skeleton.

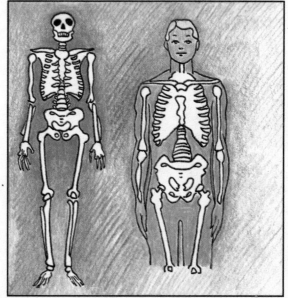

A **boy** is a male child. A **boy** will grow up to be a man.

A boy or a man is a **brother** to the other children of his father and mother.

This baby is in the **care** of its mother. She loves and looks after the baby.

A **child** is a young boy or girl. Here is a group of **children**.

The boy child or girl child of your aunt or uncle is your **cousin**.

We **cry** when we are unhappy. When we **cry**, our eyes have tears in them.

A girl is the **daughter** of her mother and father. A **daughter** is a female child.

Sometimes a **family** means two parents and their children. Sometimes our **family** means all the relatives.

A **father** is a male parent. Another name for **father** is dad.

A **friend** is someone you know and like. These two boys are good **friends**.

We enjoy playing with our friends. We have a good time. It is **fun**.

A **girl** is a female child. A **girl** will grow up to be a woman.

You are the **grandchild** of your father's parents and your mother's parents.

words about you, me and us

We have two **grandfathers**. One **grandfather** is our father's father. The other is our mother's father.

We have two **grandmothers**. One is our father's mother. Our other **grandmother** is our mother's mother.

As it **grows**, the puppy gets bigger. The puppy will **grow** up to be a dog.

Your **head** is the top of your body. Your **head** is joined by your neck to your body. Your face, your mouth, your nose, your eyes and ears are all on your **head**. Your brain is inside your **head**.

Your **heart** is in the middle of your chest. Your **heart** pumps blood round your body.

If someone falls over, we should **help** them to stand up again. They need **help**.

Home is the place where we live. **Home** can be a castle, a cottage or a caravan.

When we put our arms round someone and hold them tight, we **hug** them.

A **husband is** a married man. When a man marries a woman, he becomes her **husband**.

To show someone we love them, we touch them with our lips. We **kiss** them.

words about you, me and us

The **leg** is one of the parts of the body on which a person or an animal stands and moves about.
People have two l**egs**. Many animals have four **legs**.

We **love** our parents and our family. We like them very much. Usually we **love** animals. Sometimes we **love** dancing.

A father is a **man**. When a boy grows up, he becomes a **man**.

A **mother** is a female parent. Another name for **mother** is mum.

It is the **muscles** inside that make our bodies able to move all their different parts.

Each finger and toe has a **nail** on the end. We have five finger**nails** on each hand, and five toe**nails** on each foot.

The **name** is what we call a person, or a place or a thing. They all have **names**.

A father is a **parent** and a mother is a **parent**. Animals and plants also have **parents**.

Babies and grandparents, boys and girls, men and women, we are all **people**.

Indians and American Indians, Pakistanis and Poles, British and Brazilians – they are all **people**.

We should always say "**please**" when we ask for something. It is polite to say "**please**".

words about you, me and us

18

A **relative** is someone who belongs to the same family as ourselves. Grandparents, parents, brothers and sisters, aunts and uncles, cousins; they are all our **relatives**.

A girl or a woman is a **sister** to the other children of her parents.

Skin is the outer covering of a person, an animal, a plant or a fruit.

When we **smile**, the corners of our mouths turn up. A **smile** shows we are happy.

A boy is the **son** of a mother and father. A **son** is a male child.

We say "**thank you**" to people when they do something that pleases us. We **thank** them.

If a mother has two babies at the same time, they are **twins**. **Twins** sometimes look alike.

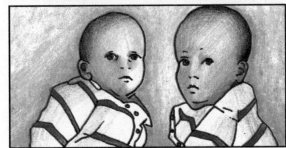

An **uncle** is either your mother's brother, or your father's brother, or your aunt's husband.

You speak and shout with your **voice**. If you sing well, you have a good **voice**.

A **wife** is a married woman. When a woman marries a man, she becomes his **wife**. All married men have **wives**.

A mother is a **woman**. When girls grow up, they become **women**.

words about you, me and us

Words about you, me and us

These are the words you have learned in the last ten pages:

age	home
arm	hug
aunt	husband
baby	kiss
blood	leg
body	love
bones	man
boy	mother
brother	muscles
care	nail
child	name
cousin	parent
cry	people
daughter	please
family	relative
father	sister
friend	skin
fun	smile
girl	son
grandchild	thank you
grandfather	twins
grandmother	uncle
grow	voice
head	wife
heart	
help	

words at home

Sometimes it is good to be **alone**. It is good to be all by yourself.

Dad wears an **apron** when he cleans our shoes. An **apron** helps to keep him clean.

My cat is **asleep** in her basket. She is not awake. She is **asleep**.

I am not asleep any more. Now I am **awake**, I am wide **awake**.

The girls are standing **back** to **back**. Mum is reaching to the **back** of the drawer.

Our **birthday** is the day on which we were born. We celebrate our **birthday** each year.

We look at pictures and read words in a **book**. **Books** are fun and very useful. I like **books**.

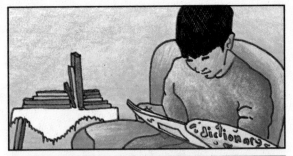

I wear **boots** on my feet. **Boots** keep our feet dry when it is muddy.

I use a **camera** to take photographs. Other **cameras** can take moving pictures.

We wear **clothes** to cover ourselves. They keep us warm in winter, or cool in summer.

Caps, anoraks, coats, boots, socks, T-shirts, underpants, jeans, ties and belts; all these are **clothes**.

Some **clothes** are simple, some **clothes** are very fancy. **Clothes** can also be called **clothing**.

words at home

I like to read a **comic**. **Comics** have rows of pictures in them called **comic** strips.

When we are asleep, we can sometimes see pictures. This is a **dream**. We are **dreaming**.

Do you **enjoy** dancing? Do you like to dance? This girl **enjoys** dancing very much.

We post letters inside **envelopes**. We write on the **envelope** the address where the letter is going.

When we are hot, we **fan** our faces. The girl **fans** herself with a **fan**.

A **flag** is a piece of cloth, or paper, with special patterns or colours on it. Countries have **flags** with different patterns.

The letter A is on the **front** of my jacket. The **front** faces forward.

My Dad is going to **give** Mum a present. He is going to hand it to her.

My teacher wears **glasses**. **Glasses** help him to see things better. **Glasses** are also called spectacles.

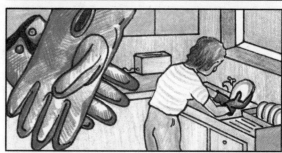

We wear **gloves** on our hands to keep them warm. **Gloves** also protect our hands.

The **hooks** behind the door are for hanging things on. My coat is on a **hook**.

My baby brother's nose tickles. His nose has an **itch**. He wants to scratch the **itch**.

words at home

In a **jigsaw** puzzle, pieces of wood or cardboard fit together to make up a picture.

The new baby brings happiness to my family. My family is full of **joy.** We are all happy.

Dad unlocks the door with a **key**. He has lots of **keys** on his **keyring**.

A **kind** person tries to help others. My sister is sharing her sweets. It is a **kind** thing to do.

I climb a **ladder** to reach the top of my slide. Firefighters and window cleaners use **ladders**.

A word is made up of **letters**. A **letter** is a message that we write to someone. I like to get **letters**.

The music is very **loud**. My friend prefers quiet music. He thinks this music is too **loud**.

My sister saved a cat from drowning. She is getting a **medal** because she is brave.

I have fallen asleep. I am having a **nap**. A **nap** is a short sleep.

The postman has a **parcel** for me. I wonder what is wrapped up in the **parcel**.

A **photograph** is a picture made with a camera. The girl is holding the boy's **photograph**.

Our clothes have **pockets** to put things in. The man's **pocket** is empty.

Mum keeps her money in her **purse**. Usually she carries her **purse** in her handbag. I put my **purse** in my pocket.

Pyjamas are a shirt and trousers for sleeping in. I wear **pyjamas** in bed.

It is **quiet** when the puppies are asleep. When it is **quiet**, there is no noise.

The **radiator** keeps my room warm. Hot water or steam passes through pipes to the **radiator**.

A **raincoat** keeps my other clothes dry when it is raining. **Raincoats** keep out water.

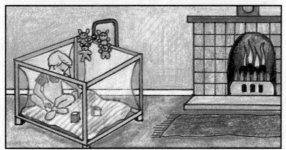

My baby brother is **safe** in the playpen. He will not come to any harm.

To keep us warm, we wear a **scarf** wrapped round our neck or round our head. **Scarves** are often colourful.

We use **scissors** to cut paper, cardboard or cloth. We must be careful with **scissors**. They are sharp.

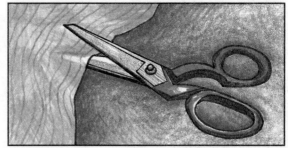

My toys are on the top **shelf**. My sister's toys are on the bottom **shelf**.

We wear **socks** on our feet. We have two feet so we wear a pair of **socks**. I have striped **socks**.

I am **sorry** I spilled the paint. I say **sorry**. I apologise.

Before I post a letter, I must put a postage **stamp** on it. I also **stamp** my foot when I am angry.

A **stool** is a small, backless chair. A foot**stool** is for putting your feet on.

Dad puts the vase on the **table** so that Laura cannot knock it over.

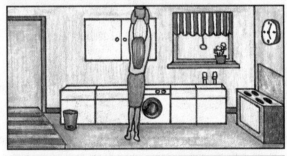

Mum stands on **tiptoe** to reach the tin. She stands on the **tips** of her **toes.**

My little sister is **tired**. She is weary. After a rest, she will not be **tired** any more.

After every meal, we brush our teeth with a **toothbrush**. We put toothpaste on the **toothbrush.**

We use a **towel** for drying or wiping ourselves. **Towels** are made of either cloth or paper.

This boy is **upside down**. **Upside down** means that the top part is at the bottom.

Teddy is in his **underwear**. He has to wear his shirt and trousers over his **underwear**.

We put flowers in a **vase** so that they will look pretty in the house.

I can tell the time on my **watch**. Most people wear a **watch** on their wrist.

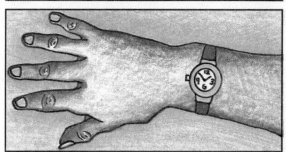

Dad has a **yawn** before he gets up every morning. Mum **yawns** when she is sleepy.

Mum opens and closes her purse with a **zipper**. She **zips** it open and shut. My purse closes with a button, not a **zipper**.

These are the words you have learned in the last ten pages:

alone	photograph
apron	pocket
asleep	purse
awake	pyjamas
back	quiet
birthday	radiator
book	raincoat
boots	safe
camera	scarf
clothes	scissors
comic	shelf
dream	socks
enjoy	sorry
envelope	stamp
fan	stool
flag	table
front	tiptoe
give	tired
glasses	toothbrush
gloves	towel
hook	upside down
itch	underwear
jigsaw	vase
joy	watch
key	yawn
kind	zipper
ladder	
letter	
loud	
medal	
nap	
parcel	

words about the house

The twins live in the same house. They have the same **address** on their letters.

The door is not closed. It is open just a little. The door is **ajar**.

The **attic** is the space in a house just under the roof. This is a room in the **attic**.

The **bathroom** is the room where we take a bath or a shower. It has a washbasin and a W.C. in it as well.

Sometimes, the **bathroom** is a room with only a W.C. and a washbasin in it.

Dad shaves in the **bathroom**. Mum has a bath there. The children like to have showers.

We go to sleep in the **bedroom**. A **bedroom** is a room with beds in it.

In Mum and Dad's **bedroom**, there is a great big bed. It is called a double bed.

In the twins' **bedroom**, there are two single beds, one above the other. These are called bunk beds.

We eat in the **dining room**. It is the room where we have our meals.

Sometimes we eat in other parts of the house.
We eat in the kitchen, or in the living room in front of the TV, but we eat our main meals in the **dining room**.

The whole family can sit round the big **dining-room** table.

A **directory** is a book that contains information. The telephone **directory** has the addresses and telephone numbers of people who have a telephone.

There are **doors** at the entrances to houses, rooms and cupboards. Sometimes a **door** slides open.

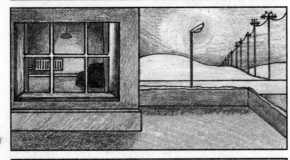

The **drawer** is open. Jack's socks are in the top **drawer** of the chest of **drawers**.

Electricity comes to us along wires. **Electricity** is a kind of energy which gives us light, heat and movement.

A **fireplace** is an opening in the wall of a room, a place to light a fire. There is a chimney above the **fireplace** for the smoke to go up to the roof.

Children must never go too near the **fireplace**.

We stand and walk on the **floor** of a room. **Floors** are hard and flat, and are often made of wood.

Beds, chairs, tables, cabinets and desks are all **furniture**. We need **furniture** in a house.

We use **glue** to stick things together. Mum uses **glue** to mend a broken vase.

We wear a dressing **gown** over our pyjamas. A teacher sometimes wears a **gown** over his jacket.

You use a **handkerchief** to wipe your eyes or your nose. **Handkerchiefs** are plain or fancy.

The cat is **indoors**, inside the house. The dog is outdoors, but wants to be **indoors**.

words about the house

The **kitchen** is the room where food is prepared and cooked. A very small **kitchen** is called a **kitchen**ette.

Mum and Dad spend a lot of time in the **kitchen**, preparing and cooking food and clearing up.

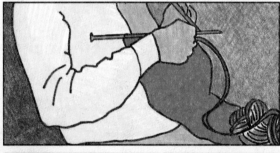

Granny is going to **knit** a scarf with the red wool. She likes **knitting.**

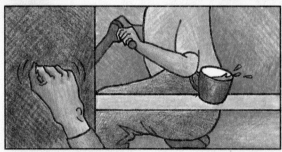

Knock on the door and someone will open it. Do not **knock** the cup over.

The **laundry** basket is full of dirty clothes. We wash our **laundry** in the washing machine.

The **lounge** is the room in the house where we relax, or **lounge** about. There are lots of comfortable chairs in the **lounge.**

We sit in the **lounge** to watch TV and read newspapers and magazines. A **lounge** can also be called a living room or a sitting room.

There are **lounges** in hotels and airports.

Sometimes my room is in a **muddle**. Everything is messed up and untidy.

We listen to music from the **music centre**. We can play records, or discs, on the record player. We can play cassettes on the cassette player. Or we can play the radio. Some **music centres** also play compact discs.

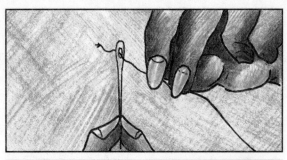

We use a **needle** for sewing. We put thread through the hole in the **needle**, the eye of the **needle.**

Here are two **odd s**ocks. We have lost the other sock of each pair.

Grandfather is **old**. He has reached **old** age. He has lived for a long time.

One book is **open**. One book is closed. His mouth is **open**. Her mouth is closed.

These children are having a **party**. It is fun to have a **party** on your birthday.

Jack has torn a hole in his trousers. Mum is sewing a **patch** over it.

It is greedy to eat all the cake. It is better just to eat a **piece** of it.

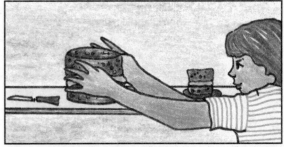

He likes to **pretend** he is hungry. He is not really hungry. He is just **pretending.**

The children are having a **quarrel**. They are fighting each other with words. They are **quarrelling**.

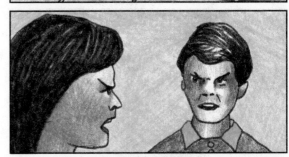

Dad uses an electric **razor** to shave his face. The **razor**blades cut off hair.

You must **remember** to take your scarf. Do not forget. **Remember** to keep it in mind.

The girl has a pretty **ribbon** in her hair. There are **ribbons** on the kite.

42

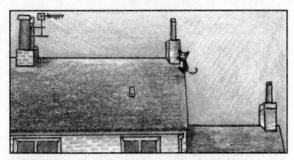

The **roof** covers the top of a house. Can you see the cat on the **roof**?

We will have to **scrub** the dirty floor. We must rub it hard to clean it.

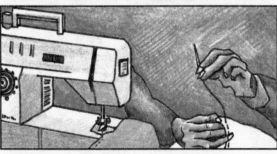

We **sew** with a needle and thread. We can **sew** by hand or with a **sewing** machine.

The gate is **shut**. We must open it. When it is **shut**, we cannot go through.

You **sneeze** when your nose tickles or you have a cold. A **sneeze** is usually noisy.

On a **telephone** we talk to people who are far away. Every **telephone** has a number.

His hair is in place. It is **tidy**. Her hair is **untidy**. It is not neat.

A **torch** helps us see in the dark. We can carry **torches** around with us.

We play with **toys**. A **toy** is a plaything. Dolls and model trains are **toys**.

When we **welcome** someone to the house, we greet them kindly. We make them feel **welcome**.

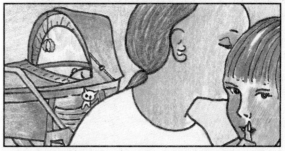

Do not speak loudly and wake the baby. Speak very quietly. Speak in a **whisper**.

If you are **young**, you have lived only for a short time. You are a **youngster**.

These are the words you have learned in the last ten pages:

address	odd
ajar	old
attic	open
bathroom	party
bedroom	patch
dining room	piece
directory	pretend
door	quarrel
drawer	razor
electricity	remember
fireplace	ribbon
floor	roof
furniture	scrub
glue	sew
gown	shut
handkerchief	sneeze
indoors	telephone
kitchen	tidy
knit	torch
knock	toys
laundry	welcome
lounge	whisper
muddle	young
music centre	
needle	

words to eat
and drink

She must eat the cake in several **bites**. She cannot eat it in one **bite**.

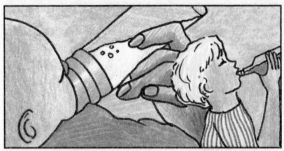

Jack is drinking orange from a **bottle**. Baby has milk in his **bottle**.

Dad bakes **bread**. He is a baker. He cuts a loaf of **bread** into two halfs.

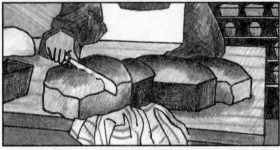

We have **breakfast** in the morning. **Breakfast** is the first meal of the day.

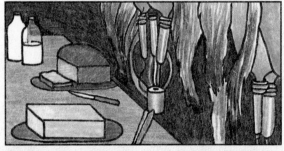

We get milk from cows. We make **butter** from milk. We eat bread and **butter**.

A **cake** is made from flour, butter, sugar and eggs. **Cakes** are good to eat.

Cheese is made from sour milk. We eat many different kinds of **cheese**.

I like **chocolate** bars, **chocolate** biscuits, **chocolate** cake and **chocolate** ice cream. I love **chocolate**!

Coffee is a drink. It is made from roasted **coffee** beans.

Cups and saucers, plates and bowls, jugs and mugs: we call all these things **crockery**.

Knives and forks, soup spoons, tea spoons and dessert spoons: we call all these things **cutlery.**

Dinner is the main meal of the day. Most people eat **dinner** in the evening.

words to eat and drink

words to eat and drink

The dog **drinks** water. The cat likes to **drink** milk. Mum likes to **drink** tea.

We **eat** when we are hungry. When we **eat**, we chew and swallow food.

Jack is eating a boiled **egg** for his breakfast. **Eggs** are laid by hens.

One pig is **fat**. One pig is thin. If we eat too much, we grow **fat**.

We eat **fish**. **Fish** live in water. Cod, haddock, sole and salmon are all **fish**.

Food is what we eat. We need **food** to keep us alive and well.

Fruit grows on trees and bushes.
Fruit is good for us..

Apples and tomatoes are **fruit**, so are grapes and grape**fruit**, oranges and lemons, melons and bananas, raspberries and strawberries.

We can eat fresh **fruit** or we can cook it. Jam is made from **fruit**.

We drink cold drinks from a **glass**. Windows are made of **glass**. So are **glasses**.

A **hamburger** is made of fried, chopped meat. Sometimes we eat **hamburgers** in buns.

Bees make **honey** inside their beehive. We eat **honey**. It is very sweet.

A **hot dog** is a hot sauságe inside a bread roll. Jack loves to eat **hot dogs**.

The cat is **hungry**. She wants something to eat. After eating, she will not be **hungry**.

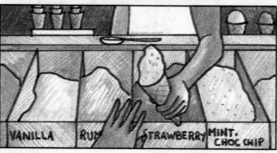

Ice cream is frozen cream and sugar. There are many different flavours of **ice cream**.

VANILLA   RUM   STRAWBERRY   MINT. CHOC CHIP

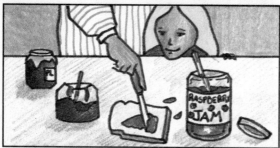

Jam is made from sugar and fruit. We spread **jam** on slices of bread.

A **jar** is a deep container made of glass and earthenware. Jam is kept in **jars**.

We keep runny liquids like milk or juice in a **jug**. A **jug** has a handle and a spout for pouring.

We put water in a **kettle**. Then we heat the **kettle** to boil the water.

A **loaf** is bread baked in one big piece. We cut slices from a **loaf** of bread.

A **lollipop** is a sweet on a stick. You can suck a **lollipop** for a long time.

Lunch is the meal we eat in the middle of the day. We **lunch** at midday.

We eat **marmalade** for breakfast. It is a special jam made from oranges, limes or lemons.

When we eat food, we have a **meal**. Breakfast, lunch, dinner and supper are **meals**.

Most people eat **meat**. **Meat** comes from animals. Beef, lamb and pork are kinds of **meat**.

We drink **milk**. **Milk** is a liquid that comes from cows, or from sheep or goats. Cats love **milk**.

A **mushroom** is a fungus, a plant without flowers, leaves or green colouring. We eat many kinds of **mushrooms**, but we must be careful as some **mushrooms** are poisonous.

We use a paper or cloth **napkin** at meals to protect our clothes from bits of food and to wipe our fingers.

Nuts have hard outsides, or shells. We eat the inside, or kernel, of a **nut**.

A **pancake** is made from flour, milk and eggs. **Pancakes** are cooked in a frying pan.

Pepper is a powder with a hot taste. It is made from dried berries of the **pepper** plant. We flavour soups, meat and vegetables with **pepper**.

A **pie** is made of meat or fruit with pastry on top or all around. **Pies** are baked in an oven.

A **pot** is a round container for cooking or storing food. We make tea in a tea**pot**.

We eat more **potatoes** than any other vegetable. Chips are made from **potatoes**. A **potato** grows underground and it has a brownish skin.

We eat **poultry**. Chickens, turkeys, geese and ducks are all **poultry**. We also eat the eggs that poultry lay.

Pudding is a sweet food that is usually eaten at the end of a meal.

In some countries, **rice** is the most important food. **Rice** is a kind of grass that grows in warm, wet places.

Salt comes from the earth and from sea water. We flavour and preserve food in **salt**.

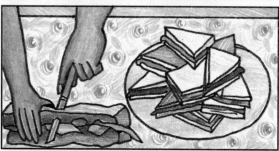

A **sandwich** is made of two slices of bread with something between, like meat or cheese.

A **sausage** is made of chopped-up meat put inside a thin skin. Most children love **sausages**.

Soup is made from water and meat or vegetables. Sometimes we begin our meal with **soup**.

Sugar is sweet. We put **sugar** in many kinds of food. Too much **sugar** is not good for our teeth and makes us fat.

Supper is the last meal of the day. Tommy Tucker had to sing for his **supper**.

We drink **tea**. We pour hot water on the leaves from **tea** plants to make **tea**.

Kitty is **thirsty**. She needs a drink. After drinking her milk, she will not be **thirsty**.

Dad is making **toast**. He is browning bread under the grill. He is **toasting** the bread.

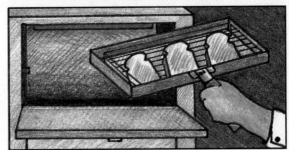

Vegetables are good for us. We eat lots of them. Onions, turnips, carrots, leeks, cabbage, peas and corn are all **vegetables**.

Nobody can live without **water**. We need **water** for drinking and washing. Never waste **water**.

These are the words you have learned in the last ten pages:

bite	loaf
bottle	lollipop
bread	lunch
breakfast	marmalade
butter	meal
cake	meat
cheese	milk
chocolate	mushroom
coffee	napkin
crockery	nut
cutlery	pancake
dinner	pepper
drink	pie
eat	pot
egg	potato
fat	poultry
fish	pudding
food	rice
fruit	salt
glass	sandwich
hamburger	sausage
honey	soup
hot dog	sugar
hungry	supper
ice cream	tea
jam	thirsty
jar	toast
jug	vegetables
kettle	water

words at play

words at play

An **acrobat** is the man or woman in a circus who does tricks on the trapeze.

The boy is an **actor**. He pretends to be someone in a play. He is **acting**.

You can hit, kick, roll or throw a **ball**. A **ball** can be round or oval.

A **balloon** will float in the air when it is blown up, or inflated.

Sometimes we use a **bat** to hit a ball. Sometimes a **bat** is a flying animal.

The girl is riding a **bicycle**. Her **bike** has two wheels, two pedals and a saddle.

The children are blowing **bubbles** with soapy water. A **bubble** floats in the air before it bursts.

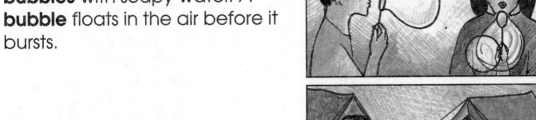

The girls are **camping** in the country. In **camp**, they sleep in tents.

The family are playing **cards**. They are all playing a **card** game.

Dad tries to **catch** the ball. If he falls in the water, he might **catch** cold.

The boys are going to run after the ball. They are going to **chase** the ball.

Going to the **cinema** is fun. We see films in the **cinema**, and sit in the dark.

A **circus** is a show inside a big tent. A **circus** has clowns and acrobats.

Monkeys **climb** trees. Boys and girls like to **climb** trees too. We **climb** the stairs at home.

A **clown** is the funny man at the circus. **Clowns** play tricks on each other.

Lots of children, a **crowd** of children, are at the party. They **crowd** around the table.

Children like to **dance**. Jack likes to **dance** to disco music. Laura loves ballet **dancing**.

The family is going for a **drive** in the car. Mum **drives** the car.

The child is hitting a **drum** with **drum**sticks. Dad is sorry the child has a **drum**.

A **fairground** has bright lights and roundabouts and all the fun of the **fair**.

Sometimes when we swim, we wear **flippers** on our feet. **Flippers** help us to swim faster.

This girl can **float** on top of the water. She lies on her back and **floats**.

We play a **game**. Hide-and-seek, catch, and snakes and ladders are all **games**.

Jack plays his **guitar**. He makes music on it. A **guitar** is a musical instrument.

The kitten tries to **hide**. She keeps out of sight. She plays **hide**-and seek.

The boy tries to **hit** the ball. He tries to strike the ball with a bat.

The boy rolls his **hoop** along the ground. The girl plays with her Hula-**Hoop**.

We **hop** by jumping about on one foot only. Many children play a game called **hop**scotch.

The **juggler** is **juggling** balls. He is keeping them all in the air at once.

Jack likes to **jump**. He is **jumping** over the box. He is a good **jumper**.

The girl gave the ball a **kick**. She hit it with her foot. She **kicked** it.

The children are flying their **kites**. A kite is made of wood and paper.

We **laugh** when we are happy. Funny things make us **laugh**. You can hear **laughter**.

A **leap** is a big jump. In **leap**frog, one child **leaps** over another one.

A **magician** can do **magic** tricks. He pulls a rabbit out of his hat. It's **magic**!

The girl wears a cat **mask** to the party. Her face is **masked**. Who is she?

When we play the guitar, we make **music**. We can hear **music** from radios, records and cassettes.

The children are making a **noise**. they are making loud sounds. They are **noisy**.

The circus is having a **parade**. The circus people are **parading** through the town.

We have a **piano** at school. When I play the **piano**, I make music on it.

The family is having a **picnic**. They are eating a meal outside on the grass.

There is an adventure **playground** in the park. We run about there and play games.

The boys are playing with **puppets**. They make a **puppet** move by pulling its strings.

The girls are running a **race**. They **race** to the line. The fastest girl wins the **race**.

It is quicker to **run** than to walk. When you **run**, you move your legs quickly.

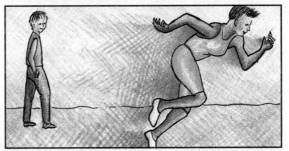

The magician is giving a **show**. He is **showing** everyone what tricks he can do.

We **sing** at school assembly. We **sing** in church. We like **singing** carols at Christmas.

It's fun to **skate** on ice. We wear our ice **skates**. Sometimes we go roller **skating**.

The children are **skipping** in the school playground. They **skip** over the **skipping**-rope.

The dog is **sliding** down the slope. The ice has made a **slide** for him.

Everybody loves to listen to a **story**. *Black Beauty* and *Bambi* are **stories**.

We **swim** by using our arms and legs to move through the water. Mark is **swimming**.

A football **team** has eleven players. They play against another **team**. Which **team** will win?

Jack has put up his **tent** in the garden. Now he is inside the **tent**.

I told Laura to **throw** the ball. She **threw** it. Now it is my **throw**.

The circus acrobat does tricks on a **trapeze**. We swing on a **trapeze** at school.

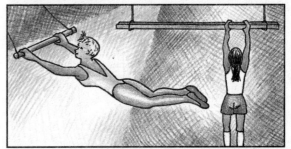

Someone has given Philip a **trumpet**. Now he is blowing loudly on his **trumpet**.

Tom is playing the **triangle**. It is called a **triangle** because it has three corners, **tri-angles**.

The girl has a toy **whistle**. She is **whistling**. The boy can **whistle** through his teeth.

Did Jack **win** the race? Jack was first. He **won** the race. He is the **winner**.

These are the words you have learned in the last ten pages:

acrobat	kick
actor	kite
ball	laugh
balloon	leap
bat	magic
bicycle	mask
bubble	music
camp	noise
cards	parade
catch	piano
chase	picnic
cinema	playground
circus	puppet
climb	race
clown	run
crowd	show
dance	sing
drive	skate
drum	skip
fairground	slide
flippers	story
float	swim
game	team
guitar	tent
hide	throw
hit	trapeze
hoop	trumpet
hop	triangle
juggler	whistle
jump	win

words at school

The boy is holding two balloons. If we **add** two balloons, then he has four. 2 **added** to 2 equals 4. 2+2=4.

We call all the letters that make words, from A to Z, the **alphabet**. The **alphabet** has 26 letters.

Do you want to know the time? **Ask** a policeman. **Ask** him to tell you.

An **atlas** is a book of maps. We use **atlases** at school to look at maps.

When the **bell** rings, it is time to go home. Teacher rings the **bell**.

Black is a colour. The words in this book are printed in **black**.

Blue is a colour. This girl is wearing a **blue** dress. Her shoes are also **blue**.

Brown is a colour. Here is a **brown** dog. The dog's kennel is also **brown**.

When we have a lot to do, we are **busy**. Bees always seem to be **busy**.

Teacher writes in **chalk** on the board. Usually he uses white **chalk**. **Chalk** makes dust.

Our **class** is Primary II. We sit in a **class**room. Mrs Smith is our **class** teacher.

Playing with **clay** is great fun. It is messy. We make things out of **clay**.

A **clock** shows you what time it is. Alarm **clocks** wake us up in the morning.

A **compass** can show us which way to go. The **compass** needle always points to the north.

Computers at school help us to learn. We have a home **computer** for work and play.

Teacher told us to **copy** the words. We must **copy** the words into our books.

Jack sits at a **desk** at school. Dad works at a **desk** in his office.

If we have 1 apple and 4 children, we must **divide** the apple into pieces.
This apple will **divide** into 8 pieces. How many will each child get?

If you **double** your money, you have twice as much as before. **Double** 5 is 10.

When you **draw** something, you make a **drawing**, or picture, of it with a pen or pencil.

I do not understand. Please **explain** it to me. Make it clear. Give me an **explanation**.

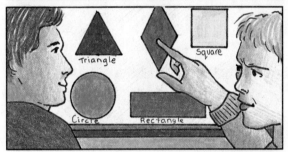

Green is a colour. Grass is **green**. So are leaves. Dad's car is **green**.

Grey is a colour. Grandfather has lots of **grey** hair. Lots of winter days are **grey**.

Here is a **group** of children. Many people together are called a **group**.

A **gymnasium** or **gym** is a room at school where we do exercises to make our bodies healthy.

Cut the cake into two equal parts. We have **halved** it. We will have **half** each.

The whole school meets in the big **hall**. We have morning assembly in the **hall**.

This girl's **hobby** is collecting stamps. **Hobbies** are something to do to pass the time.

Your **initials** are the first letters of your names. **J**ohn **W**illiam **S**mith's **initials** are JWS.

We go to school to **learn** things. We find out about reading. We are **learning** to read.

We learn many **lessons** at school. Each **lesson** is something we must learn.

The alphabet has 26 **letters**. A is the first **letter** and Z is the last **letter**.

Something that we throw away is called **litter**. We must put it in the **litter** bin.

A **magnet** pulls iron towards it. We can pick up pins with a **magnet**.

A **map** is a drawing which shows countries, rivers, mountains, seas and cities. This is a **map** of Australia.

We **measure** how long, deep, wide or large something is. We also **measure** how much there is of something.

Jack gave the wrong answer. He made a **mistake**, an error. He was **mistaken**.

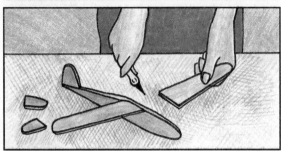

The boy is making a **model** aircraft. A **model** is a small copy.

We learn to **multiply** at school. If we **multiply** 3 by 3, the answer is 9.

A **name** is what someone or something is called. This boy is called Jack. His **name** is Jack.

The teacher has put a **notice** on the board. We must pay attention to the **notice**.

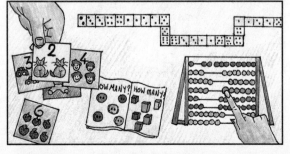

We count things or people in **numbers**. We **number** them. A **number** tells us how many there are.

Opposite means as different as possible. Cold is **opposite** to hot. Big and little are **opposites**. Up is **opposite** to down.

A **pattern** is the way in which colours and shapes are arranged. This dress has a pretty **pattern** on it.

A **quarter** is one of four equal parts. Fifteen minutes is a **quarter** of an hour. Two **quarters** are a half.

The teacher asks a **question** to find out if Laura knows the answer. He **questions** her.

The boys **queue** at the bus stop. They stand in a line. They form a **queue**.

I can **read** writing and printing. I **read** the words. I understand their meaning.

Red is a colour. Ripe tomatoes are **red**. We colour things **red** to warn of danger.

Teacher keeps a **register**. A **register** is a list of the children in a class.

The boy has a **satchel** on his back. He carries his school things in his **satchel**.

School is the place where we learn lessons. We learn to read and write at **school**.

Laura has a **set** of crayons, one of each colour. A **set** of things belong together.

Subtract means to take away from. **Subtract** one egg from six eggs and five eggs remain.

We add things together to get the **sum**. The **sum** of 2 and 3 is 5.

The **teacher** is showing the boy how to read and write. He is **teaching** him.

We have a **test** at school to see how much we have learned. We are **tested**.

White is a colour. The paper in this book is **white**. Jack has a **white** shirt.

Andrew is **writing** his name. He uses a pen to **write** the letters that make the words.

Yellow is a colour. Butter is **yellow**, so are lemons. **Yellow** is a bright, happy colour.

These are the words you have learned in the last ten pages:

add	lesson
alphabet	letters
ask	litter
atlas	magnet
bell	map
black	measure
blue	mistake
brown	model
busy	multiply
chalk	name
class	notice
clay	number
clock	opposite
compass	pattern
computer	quarter
copy	question
desk	queue
divide	read
double	red
draw	register
explain	satchel
green	school
grey	set
group	subtract
gymnasium	sum
half	teacher
hall	test
hobby	white
initials	write
learn	yellow

words about animals

An **animal** is anything alive that is not a plant. Monkeys, goats, grasshoppers and goldfish are **animals**.

Badgers live undergound and come out at night. A **badger** has short legs and thick, grey fur.

Bears are large and have thick fur. A **bear** hibernates, which means that he sleeps through the winter.

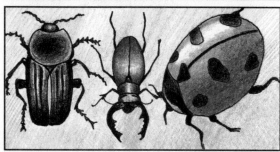

A **beetle** is an insect with hard, glossy, front wings and six legs. A ladybird is a kind of **beetle**.

Birds have wings and feathers and they lay eggs. Most **birds** can fly.

Butterflies are insects with slender bodies and four large wings. The wings of a **butterfly** are usually brightly coloured.

Camels have one or two humps. A **camel** lives in the desert and can carry heavy loads.

A **canary** is a small, yellow songbird which is often kept as a pet.

A small, furry **cat** is a good pet. Lions, tigers and leopards are big **cats**.

Caterpillars are long and soft. A **caterpillar** is a young butterfly or moth which has just hatched from its egg.

Cows are fully grown female cattle. A **cow** eats grass and gives us milk to drink.

Crocodiles are reptiles with thick skins and sharp teeth. A **crocodile** lives in hot, wet places.

Deer are shy animals that can move very fast. Male **deer** are called stags. They have antlers on their heads.

Dinosaurs are no longer alive. They lived millions of years ago. Some **dinosaurs** were very big.

A **dog** is our friend. Some **dogs** are pets. Other **dogs**, like sheep**dogs**, work very hard.

A **duck** is a swimming bird, with a flat bill and webbed feet. **Ducks** say, "quack, quack".

Elephants are the largest animals on land. An **elephant** has a long nose which is called a trunk.

Some **fish** live in ponds and rivers, in freshwater. Other **fish** live in the sea, in saltwater.

Foxes are very clever. A **fox** has a bushy tail, and hunts for food at night.

Frogs live near streams and ponds. A **frog** moves by taking big hops. Tadpoles are baby **frogs**.

A **giraffe** has a very long neck and legs. **Giraffes** are the tallest animals. They live in Africa.

A **goat** has hoofs. Some also have horns and a beard. We get milk from **goats**.

People have **goldfish** as pets and keep them in a tank or bowl. **Goldfish** are a golden colour.

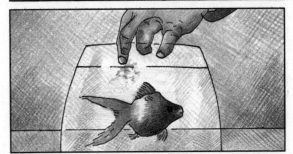

A **grasshopper** is a small insect with wings and strong back legs. It is a great jumper.

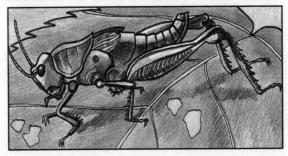

A **hamster** is like a large mouse with big cheek pouches. People have **hamsters** as charming pets and keep them in cages.

Hens often live in farmyards. They lay eggs. A young **hen** is a chicken.

The huge **hippopotamus** lives in Africa. It has a thick skin. Its name means "river horse".

The **horse** is our friend. We ride **horses**, and they also work for us. They can pull carts.

The body of an **insect** is in three parts. It has six legs. Flies, bees and grasshoppers are **insects**.

Kangaroos are wild animals that live in Australia. Mother **kangaroo** carries her baby in a pouch.

A **leopard** is a large animal of the cat family. It has black spots.

The **lion** is called "the king of beasts". He is a large, strong cat with a loud roar.

Monkeys are very like people. A **monkey** is intelligent, active, and full of mischief.

A **mouse** has long whiskers, sharp teeth and a long tail. Many **mice** can do much damage.

The **octopus** lives in the sea. It has a soft body and eight arms with suckers on them.

The **ostrich** is the largest living bird. **Ostriches** cannot fly, but they can run very fast.

Owls are birds with large eyes. They can see in the dark. We talk about "a wise **owl**".

The **panda** is a rare animal and looks like a black and white bear.
Pandas live in China.

A **parrot** is a bird with a strong, hooked bill and brightly coloured feathers. Some **parrots** can talk.

Male **peacocks** have such beautiful fantails that we say someone is "as proud as a **peacock**".

A **penguin** is a black and white sea bird. **Penguins** swim in cold seas. They cannot fly.

Pets are animals, like cats and dogs, that we keep as favourites and treat with love and kindness.

A **pig** lives on a farm in a **pig**sty. **Pigs** have curly tails and flat noses.

A **rabbit** has long, soft ears. Wild **rabbits** live in burrows, pet **rabbits** live in a hutch.

Reindeer live in the frozen north and have large antlers. **Reindeer** pull Santa Claus's sleigh.

Reptiles are cold-blooded animals. A tortoise is a **reptile**; so are crocodiles, lizards and snakes.

A **rhinoceros,** or **rhino**, is a large, heavy animal with one or two horns on its nose.

A **seal** is a warm-blooded, furry animal that lives in the sea and eats fish.

words about animals

We make wool from the fleece, or coat, of a **sheep**. A young **sheep** is a lamb.

A **snail** has a shell and moves very slowly. It lives in its shell, so it carries its house on its back.

A **snakes** is long and thin. **Snakes** have a scaly skin and no legs. Some **snake**bites are poisonous.

A **spider** has eight legs. It spins a **spider's** web to catch insects for food.

A **squirrel** has a long bushy tail and lives in trees. Some **squirrels** are red, some are grey.

A **swan** is a large, graceful water bird with a long, curving neck. A young **swan** is called a cygnet.

A **tiger** is large and fierce. It has yellowish fur with black stripes. **Tigers** live in Asia but are rare.

A **tortoise** has a thick, hard shell. **Tortoises** move very slowly and live a long time.

A **vet** is an animal doctor. We take sick animals to the veterinary surgeon, the **vet**.

A **whale** is the largest animal alive. **Whales** are intelligent and warm-blooded like us. People have killed many **whales** for their oil.

The **zebra** is like a striped horse. We cross the road at a **zebra** crossing.

A **zoo** is a park where people can go to see wild animals, especially rare ones.

words about animals

These are the words you have learned in the last ten pages:

animal

badger

bear

beetle

bird

butterfly

camel

canary

cat

caterpillar

cow

crocodile

deer

dinosaurs

dog

duck

elephant

fish

fox

frog

giraffe

goat

goldfish

grasshopper

hamster

hen

hippopotamus

horse

insect

kangaroo

leopard

lion

monkey

mouse

octopus

ostrich

owl

panda

parrot

peacock

penguin

pets

pig

rabbit

reindeer

reptile

rhinoceros

seal

sheep

snail

snake

spider

squirrel

swan

tiger

tortoise

vet

whale

zebra

zoo

words doing things

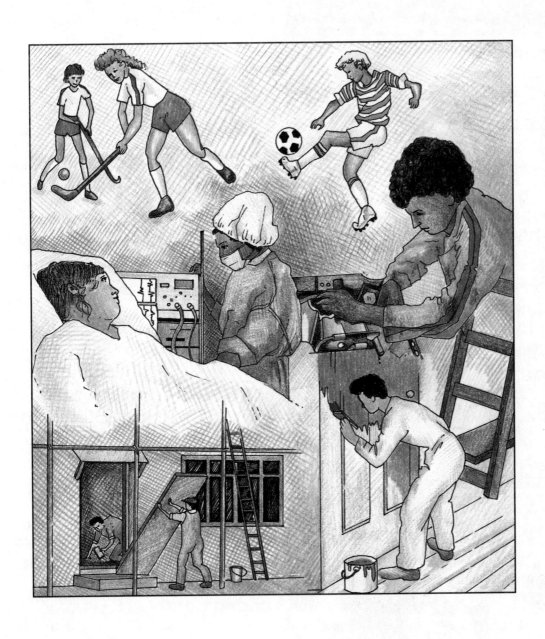

An **air stewardess** looks after you when you are travelling in an aircraft.

Laura is an **artist**. She is good at painting pictures. She is **artistic**.

A **baker** makes bread, cakes and pies. He **bakes** them. He cooks them in an oven.

We keep money in a **bank**. The person who looks after the **bank** is a **banker**.

At a wedding, the woman who is getting married is the **bride**. The man she marries is the **bridegroom**.

A **builder** is someone who **builds** houses or other **buildings**. These are **built** by **builders**.

A **bulldozer** is a tractor with a front blade that levels the ground. **Bulldozers** help to build roads.

A **church** is a place where people pray to God. Most towns have **churches**.

Thousands of people live and work in a **city**. **Cities** are much bigger than towns.

Jack is the **cook** tonight. He is making the dinner. He is **cooking** it.

Cowboys look after the cattle, or cows. A **cowboy** wears a big hat and boots.

A **crane** is a machine with a long, swinging arm. **Cranes** can lift very heavy objects.

words doing things

Laura is **crossing** the road. She is going **across** the road. She uses the zebra **crossing**.

Dentists look after our teeth. We should visit the **dentist** often if we want healthy, shining teeth.

If someone is ill, a **doctor** helps them to get better. **Doctors** look after sick people.

A **diver** goes down deep under the water. Sometimes **divers** wear special **diving** suits.

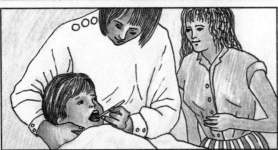

An **electrician** works with **electrical** things that give us light and heat.

A **factory** is a building where things are made. People and machines work in **factories**.

Food is grown on a **farm**, and **farm** animals are kept there. **Farmers** run **farms**.

Jack has a **fever**. He is hot and feels **feverish**. He is sick. Call the doctor.

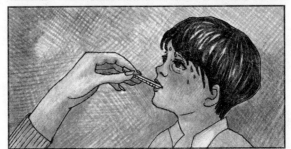

A **firefighter** fights **fires** and puts them out. **Firefighters** race to the fire in **fire** engines.

Hairdressers take care of people's hair. A **hairdresser** will shampoo hair, cut it and style it.

Hockey is a game for two teams. It is played on a field or on ice. A **hockey** stick is used to hit the ball.

Lots of people love **horse-riding**. Some race horses, some jump horses, some just ride.

People who are sick are cared for in a **hospital**. Doctors and nurses work in **hospitals**.

A **hotel** is a building with rooms where people can stay when they are travelling. Most towns have **hotels**.

Books are kept in a **library**. People go to **libraries** to borrow the books and to study.

A **machine** works for people. This book was made by machines. Cars, computers and cranes are **machines**.

Things are bought and sold at a **market**. **Markets** can be in an open space or inside buildings.

Mechanics work with tools, and make, use or mend machines. A car **mechanic** fixes cars.

We take **medicine** to make us better when we are ill. Our doctor tells us what **medicines** to take.

A **miner** works underground. **Miners** work in **mines**, digging for coal, diamonds and gold. **Mining** is dangerous work.

Most people earn **money** by working. We need **money** to buy things like food and clothes.

Nurses are men and women who take care of sick people. They **nurse** the sick.

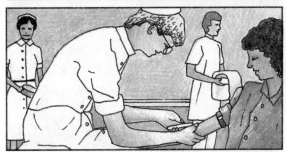

Most days Dad goes to the **office**. The **office** is the place where he works.

A **painter** may **paint** pictures. House **painters paint** insides and outsides of houses. This man is **painting** the ceiling.

A **pilot** flies an aircraft. The people who steer ships into port are also called **pilots**.

When our water pipe was leaking, the **plumber** mended it. A **plumber** stops taps from dripping.

The **police** are men and women who catch people who do wrong things, the people who break the law.

Pollution makes the air dirty. The exhaust from Dad's car **pollutes** the air and makes it dirty.

A **professor** teaches people after they leave school. **Professors** teach in a college or university.

A **sailor** works on a ship. Some ships have engines, some have only **sails**. All ships need **sailors**.

These men **sell** fruit. People buy the fruit they are **selling**. They give the men money for the fruit.

Mum is **shopping**. She goes to the **shop** to buy things. Is she **shopping** for sweets?

Baby is not well. Baby feels **sick**. Doctor will come to see the **sick** baby.

The class **signs** teacher's birthday card. They write their names on it. They **sign** it.

Dad plays **snooker**. **Snooker** is a game played with coloured balls on a big, green table.

The men and women who guard our country are **soldiers**. A **soldier** wears special clothes called a uniform.

words doing things

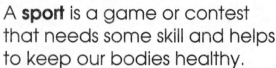

A **sport** is a game or contest that needs some skill and helps to keep our bodies healthy.

Sports can take place indoors, like basketball, or outdoors, like cricket and football.

Running is a **sport** that you do by yourself. You need 22 people to play the **sport** of football. **Sport** is fun and good for us.

Things are kept in a **store**. They are **stored** there. A super**store** is a big shop.

Streets have houses and traffic in them. A **street** is a road in a town. Cross the **street** carefully.

A **sweeper** is the person who keeps our streets clean. **Sweepers sweep** up all the litter.

Table tennis is a sport we play on a wooden table with a bat and a ball. **Table tennis** is also called "Ping-Pong".

Two or four people can play **tennis**. **Tennis** is a sport that is played on grass or on a hard court, indoors or outdoors.

Lots of people live in **towns**. A **town** is smaller than a city but bigger than a village.

Not many people live in a **village**. A **village** is smaller than a town.

How much do you **weigh**? How heavy are you? We **weigh** things to discover their **weight**.

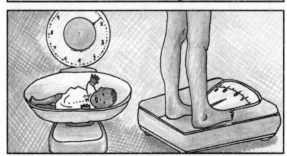

An **X-ray** is a picture of the inside of our bodies. Doctor **X-rays** us to see if all is well.

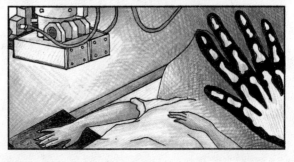

These are the words you have learned in the last ten pages:

air stewardess
artist
baker
bank
bride, bridegroom
builder
bulldozer
church
city
cook
cowboy
crane
crossing
dentist
doctor
diver
electrician
factory
farm
fever
firefighter
hairdresser
hockey
horse-riding
hospital
hotel
library
machine
market

mechanic
medicine
miner
money
nurse
office
painter
pilot
plumber
police
pollution
professor
sailor
sell
shopping
sick
sign
snooker
soldier
sport
store
street
sweeper
table tennis
tennis
town
village
weigh
X-ray

words going places

An **aircraft** is a machine that flies through the air. **Aircraft** have engines and wings. An aeroplane is an **aircraft** and so is a helicopter.

Aircraft take off and land at an **airport**. We take a plane at the **airport**.

Ambulances take sick people to hospital. An **ambulance** is a white van with a loud siren.

When did you **arrive**? When did you get here? You **arrived** yesterday. You got here yesterday.

An **astronaut** travels in space. The first people to stand on the moon were **astronauts.**

Boats go on water. A **boat** is smaller than a ship. Sometimes you row a **boat**.

To get to the other side of the river, you have to cross over the **bridge**. The river is **bridged** by it.

Lots of people travel to different places in **buses**. This is the school **bus**.

The girl can **carry** her cat. She is **carrying** it. The cat is being **carried**.

The person steering a car, a bus or a lorry is the **driver**. Here is a bus **driver**.

School begins at nine. Jack arrives at eight. Jack is before the usual time. He is **early**.

We **enter** through the door. We go in through the door. The door is the **entrance**.

We go out through that door. We **exit** that way. It is the **exit**.

It is **far**. It is not near. It is distant. It is **far** away.

Aircraft go **fast**. They go very quickly. How **fast** are they? How quick are they?

A ship called a **ferry** takes us from one side of the water to the other. Many **ferries** cross the English Channel.

After school, where do you **go**? I walk from school to my home. I **go** home.

Uncle John is leaving. Say "**goodbye**" to him. We say "**goodbye**" when we part from someone.

The **guide** is taking people around the castle. She is **guiding** them.

A **helicopter** is an aircraft without wings. A **helicopter** has a big propeller on top of it.

"**Hello**, Jack." **Hello** is a greeting. We greet Jack by saying "**hello**" when we meet.

Mum is **in** the car. Dad is not **in** the car. Dad gets **in**to the car.

The hamsters are **inside** the cage. Baby loves hamsters. Baby wants to be **inside** as well.

Jack was not here for lunch. He was **late**. Laura was here at the right time. She was not **late**.

Laura must **leave** now. She must go away. It is time for Laura to **leave**.

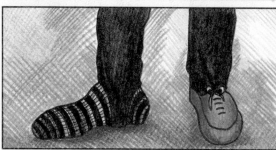

One side of you is your **left** side. This girl is wearing only her **left** shoe on her **left** foot.

Motorcar is the full name of a car. We drive along the road in a **motorcar**.

Motorbikes have two wheels and an engine. They are also called motorcycles. They can travel fast. This policeman rides a **motorbike**.

The men **move** the box. They put it in a different place. The box is **moved**.

We are **near** the village. We are close to the village. The village is **nearby**.

The dog is in the house. The dog wants to go **out** through the door. **Out** you go, dog!

The **outside** of the car is dirty. We must wash the **outside** of the car.

Sometimes **pigeons** carry messages for people. The carrier **pigeon** has a message tied to its leg.

Boats and ships load and unload things in a **port**, where there are cranes to help. A **port** is also a harbour.

A train stops at a **platform**. People wait on the **platform** to get on the train.

The boy tries to **pull** the dog. The dog will not move. The boy **pulls** him.

The girl has to **push** the dog. The dog will not move. The girl **pushes** him.

The donkey is giving the boy a **ride**. Afterwards the boy will **ride** home in Dad's car.

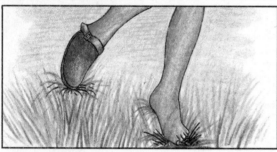

One side of you is your **right** side. This girl is wearing only her **right** shoe on her **right** foot.

A **road** is a way between places. Buses, cars, lorries and bicycles travel on **roads**.

Which way will you go? One **route** is prettier. The other **route** is quicker.

Aircraft take off from and land on a **runway** at the airport. **Runways** are firm and level.

Sometimes a boat has a **sail**. The wind blowing into the **sails** blows the boat along.

A **ship** is a big boat. Some **ships** sail round the world. Battle**ships** fight sea battles.

A **signpost** tells you which route to take to get to a place. **Signposts** have arms.

The express train is fast. The old train goes **slowly**. It is **slow**, not fast.

A **spaceship** travels in space. Astronauts travel to the moon in a **spaceship**.

The car will not **start**. It will not begin to move. We cannot **start** the car.

The train stops at all **stations**. People get on a train at one **station** and off at another.

The red light means **stop**. We must not go on. Dad must **stop** the car.

A **submarine** is a ship that travels under the sea. Some **submarines** stay underwater for months.

A **taxi** is a special car. You pay the **taxi** driver to drive you somewhere.

Trains and trams move along on **tracks**. A **track** is two lines of rails on which the wheels turn.

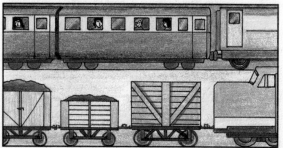

Trains move along railway lines, or tracks. A **train** carries people in carriages and freight in wagons.

A **truck**, or lorry, carries heavy loads along a road. Most **trucks** are very big and strong.

A **tunnel** is a route under the ground or underwater. Roads and railways go through **tunnels.** Some **tunnels** are very long.

A **van** is a small lorry, or truck. The Post Office **van** carries letters and parcels.

When we **walk**, we put one foot in front of the other. These boys are **walking**.

Cars, trucks and trains all move on **wheels**. A bike has two **wheels**. A **wheel** is round.

A **yacht** is a boat with sails. It is fun to go **yachting**. Some people have races in **yachts**.

These are the words you have learned in the last ten pages:

aircraft	out
airport	outside
ambulance	pigeon
arrive	port
astronaut	platform
boat	pull
bridge	push
bus	ride
carry	right
driver	road
early	route
enter	runway
exit	sail
far	ship
fast	signpost
ferry	slow
go	spaceship
goodbye	start
guide	station
helicopter	stop
hello	submarine
in	taxi
inside	track
late	train
leave	truck
left	tunnel)
motorcar	van
motorbike	walk
move	wheel
near	yacht

words on holiday

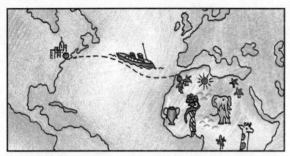

Abroad means outside our own country. A holiday **abroad** is a holiday in another country.

The **band** is playing on the beach. A **band** is a group of people making music.

A **beach** is the flat, sandy part beside the sea. Sometimes the **beaches** have pebbles instead of sand.

A **candle** burns and gives light. We light **candles** at special times, and we put them on birthday cakes.

A **canoe** is a narrow little boat that is pointed at both ends. Jack paddles his **canoe** through the water.

On someone's birthday we make a special fuss of them. We **celebrate** it with a **celebration** or a party.

We celebrate **Christmas** on December 25th each year. It is **Christmas** Day, the birthday of Jesus Christ. Christians go to church to celebrate the birthday.

Christmas is a holiday in our country. We often have a **Christmas** tree inside the house. We make it pretty with coloured lights and decorations. We give each other **Christmas** presents.

Laura must be careful on top of the **cliff**. The **cliff** face goes down to the sea.

Jack has found a **crab** on the beach. **Crabs** have a hard shell, eight legs and two strong claws.

We have **crackers** at parties. It is fun to pull a **cracker** until it goes "bang".

We go for a **cruise** in a ship or a boat. A **cruise** is a holiday on water. We **cruise** around.

When we **decorate** something we make it prettier. We hang **decorations** on a Christmas tree.

We must **delay** our holiday. We must put it off until later. **Delays** make us late.

When we **depart**, we go away. The train is about to **depart** from the station.

Donkeys are like small horses with long ears. We have **donkey** rides on the beach.

It is fun to **dress up**. Jack likes to **dress up** in an old army uniform.

Easter is a holiday in our country. We give each other chocolate **Easter** eggs.

The children are having a **fancy dress** party. The boy is wearing a **fancy dress** costume.

Firecrackers, skyrockets and other **fireworks** make a loud noise and give us a colourful, sparkling show.

We can go **fishing** in the sea or in ponds or rivers. We **fish** with a net or a rod and line.

Swimming in the sea is **free**. There is no charge. We are **free** to swim in the sea if we want to.

Jack tries to **frighten** Laura. He jumps out and gives her a **fright**. She is **frightened**.

The boy dresses up as a **ghost**. Granny is frightened. She is as white as a **ghost**.

Our **guest** is someone who comes to visit us. We are **guests** in a hotel.

Guy is a word that some people use for a boy. Here are two **guys** and a girl.

October 31st is **Hallowe'en**. We dress up as witches and ghosts and put candles inside pumpkins. **Hallowe'en** is the evening before All Saints' Day.

We go **hiking** over the countryside. These **hikers** carry clothes and food in their backpacks.

We rest from work on a **holiday**. A **holiday** can last for one day, or for several weeks.

We **label** our suitcases. We tie on a **label** with our name and address on it.

It is fun to have a **lantern** in the tent. The **lantern** has a candle in it that burns and gives us light.

Every year we celebrate the **New Year**. We wish each other "Happy **New Year**". **New Year's Day** is January 1st, the first day of the year. We like to have the whole family together for a **New Year** party.

We **pack** our suitcase for our holiday. We put our clothes in it. Then we **unpack** our suitcases when we arrive.

Laura is having a **paddle**. The water only reaches her ankles. Jack **paddles** his canoe.

Everyone wears a **paper hat** at the party. Mum's **paper hat** is a pretty crown.

The family goes **pony-trekking**. They go for a long ride, or **trek**, on ponies.

A **postcard** is for posting to friends. On one side of the **postcard** is a picture. On the other side we write a message.

We give people **presents**. We make them a **present** of something. Everyone likes to get **presents** at Christmas.

A **restaurant** is a place where we go to eat. In a **restaurant** other people cook a meal for us , and we pay them.

We play with **sand** on the beach or in **sand** boxes. We make **sand**castles.

A **seagull** is a large sea bird with a loud cry. **Seagulls** are very greedy.

We find pretty **seashells** beside the sea. **Seashells** are empty **shells** in which little sea animals once lived.

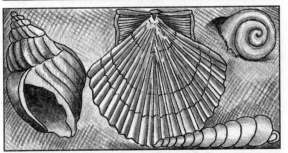

On holiday, we see the **sights**. We go **sight**seeing. Churches, mountains and waterfalls are **sights**.

Dad loves to **ski**. He **skis** on snow-covered mountainsides. We have **skiing** holidays with him.

Laura jumps into the water. She makes a **splash**. Her friends enjoy **splashing** about.

words on holiday

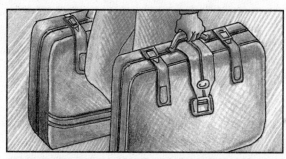

When we go on holiday, we pack all our clothes in a **suitcase**. We carry our **suitcases**.

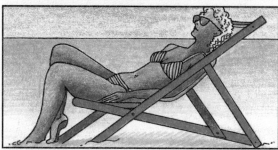

Mum likes to lie on the beach and **sunbathe**. She gets a tan when she **sunbathes**.

The girl is wearing **sunglasses**. **Sunglasses** protect her eyes from the sun. Bright sun hurts eyes.

Granny is **surprised**. She did not expect to see Jack. Jack has given her a **surprise**.

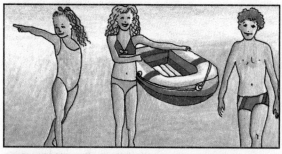

The children are wearing **swimsuits**. We wear **swimsuits** to swim in the sea.

The boy is on a **swing**. He is **swinging** up and down, high in the air.

Mum has a good **tan**. The sun has made her body brown. She is **tanned**.

We buy a **ticket** to go into the cinema. We buy it at the **ticket box**.

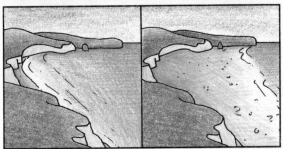

At high **tide**, the sea comes right up the beach. At low **tide**, it is far out.

For our holiday, we went on a **tour**. We were **tourists**, travelling from place to place.

On St **Valentine's** Day, February 14th, we send a card called a **valentine** to someone we love.

The **waiter** brings us a meal in a restaurant. He serves us. He **waits** on us.

These are the words you have learned in the last ten pages:

abroad

band

beach

candle

canoe

celebrate

Christmas

cliff

crab

cracker

cruise

decoration

delay

depart

donkey

dress up

Easter

fancy dress

fireworks

fishing

free

frighten

ghost

guest

guy

Hallowe'en

hiking

holiday

label

lantern

New Year

pack

paddle

paper hat

pony trekking

postcard

present

restaurant

sand

seagull

seashells

sights

ski

splash

suitcase

sunbathe

sunglasses

surprise

swimsuit

swing

tan

ticket

tide

tourist

valentine

waiter

words outdoors

A **barn** is the building where a farmer keeps cows. He stores hay in the **barn**.

Blossom is the flower of a fruit tree or bush. Apple trees in **blossom** are beautiful.

We burn our garden rubbish on a **bonfire**. Dried autumn leaves make a great **bonfire**.

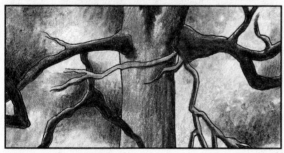

A **branch** grows out from the trunk of a tree. Trees have many **branches**. Big **branches** are boughs.

A **brook** is a small stream. We can sail toy boats and paddle in a **brook**.

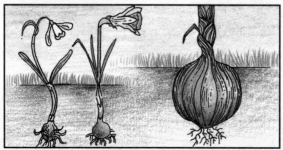

A **bulb** is the underground part from which some plants grow. Onions are **bulbs**.

A **cave** is a hole underground or in the side of a hill. Thousands of years ago, people lived in **caves**. Bears sleep in **caves**.

A **cottage** is a small house. Some old **cottages** have thatched roofs made of straw.

We find fresh air, green fields and trees in the **country**. Farms are in the **countryside**.

Milk and cream are kept in a **dairy**. We make butter and cheese in a **dairy**.

A long, narrow **ditch** is dug to carry water away, so the land is not flooded.

Echoes are repeated sounds. If you shout near a hill, you will hear an **echo** bouncing back.

Farmers put **fences** around their fields. They **fence** them. The horse is jumping over the **fence**.

Farms are divided into **fields**. Corn grows in one **field**. Animals are kept in another **field**.

A **forest** has thousands of trees. Robin Hood and his Merry Men lived in Sherwood **Forest**.

Dad grows vegetables, fruit and flowers in the **garden**. He works in the **garden**. He does the **gardening**. He is the **gardener**.
  Some **gardens** have pools with goldfish, and wooden seats and swings. Some **gardens** are so lovely that people even pay to look round them.

Grass grows on the ground. Grass is green. Cows eat grass. Long dry grass makes hay.

The harvest is what we get from a year's work growing things. On farms, autumn is harvest time.

Hay is grass that has been cut and dried for animal food. Farmers make hay.

A hill is higher than the land round about it. Jack and Jill went up the hill.

The horizon is where we see the land or sea meet the sky. We cannot see over the horizon.

A hut is a small wooden house. We keep garden chairs and tools in a hut.

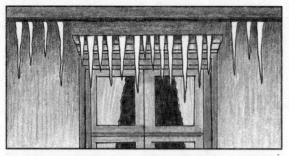

An **icicle** is a long drip of frozen water. **Icicles** melt when the weather gets warmer.

Ivy is a climbing plant with shiny green leaves. Often **ivy** clings to trees and house walls.

The **kerb** is the edge of the pavement. We must wait at the **kerb** before crossing the road.

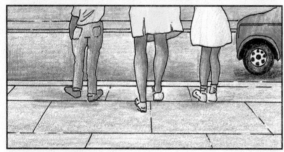

A **lake** is water with land all round it. A **lake** is larger than a pond.

A **lane** is a narrow road in the country. Motorways are divided into **lanes**.

A **leaf** grows on a tree or plant. In autumn, the **leaves** fall off most trees.

A **lighthouse** is a tall building beside the sea. Its bright light warns ships of danger.

In the country, **meadows** are fields of grassy land. Cows and horses feed in a **meadow**.

Moss is the small green plant growing on the ground, rocks and trees, like a carpet. **Mosses** like damp places.

Mountains are very high hills. In winter, a **mountain** top will be covered by snow and ice.

After the rain, we get **muddy** walking in the fields. **Muddy** earth is wet and sticky.

Everything in the world not made by people is called **nature**. We marvel at **nature's** wonders.

An **oasis** is a place in the desert where plants can grow because there is water.

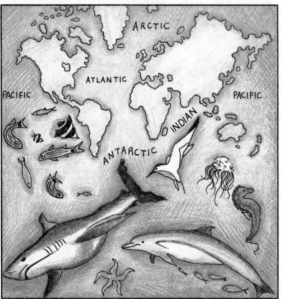

Saltwater **oceans**, or seas, cover almost three-quarters of the surface of the world.
There are five **oceans**. They are called the Atlantic, Pacific, Indian, Arctic and Antarctic **Oceans**. Great Britain is on the edge of the Atlantic **Ocean**.

Orchards are gardens full of fruit trees. Apples, pears and plums are grown in an **orchard**.

Parks have grass, flowers and trees. Sometimes a **park** also has a pond and a playground.

A **peak** is the very top of any mountain. A **peak** is also a mountain that stands all alone.

A **plant** is anything alive that is not an animal. **Plants** grow in the ground and in water.

A **pond** is water with land all around. A **pond** is much smaller than a lake.

We move a **pump** handle up and down to **pump** water from a well in the ground.

We get stones for building things from a **quarry**. Stones are **quarried** from the face of the rock.

A **river** can be hundreds of miles long and miles wide. **Rivers** flow towards the sea or ocean.

A **rock** is a large stone. **Rock** is very hard. Some **rocks** are bigger than hills.

The **root** of a plant is underground. **Roots** keep a plant in place. Plants feed through their **roots**.

Most plants grow from **seeds**. We plant **seeds** and cover them with earth, then they grow.

A **stream** is a small river. The **stream** of water is always moving. It **streams** along.

Tools help us to work. A rake is a gardener's **tool**. Saws are **tools** for woodworkers.

A **tractor** can have huge wheels or tracks. **Tractors** can move easily over rough ground. Farmers use **tractors**.

A **valley** is the low ground between hills. Rivers are often at the bottom of **valleys**.

A **wave** is a moving bump on the surface of water. **Waves** make a boat go up and down. Surfers ride the **waves**.

A **weathervane** is on top of a building to show us which way the wind is blowing.

Weeds are wild plants. Gardeners hate **weeds**. They pull them out. They **weed** the garden.

A **well** is a deep hole that is dug in the ground to find water, oil or gas.

Windmills often pump water. Wind blows the **windmill's** arms, or sails, round to work the pump.

Something we do because we have to is **work**. Most people **work** for a living. Some **work** outdoors, some indoors and some underground.

These are the words you have learned in the last ten pages:

barn	meadow
blossom	moss
bonfire	mountain
branch	muddy
brook	nature
bulb	oasis
cave	ocean
cottage	orchard
country	park
dairy	peak
ditch	plant
echo	pond
fence	pump
field	quarry
forest	river
garden	rock
grass	root
harvest	seeds
hay	stream
hill	tool
horizon	tractor
hut	valley
icicle	wave
ivy	weathervane
kerb	weed
lake	well
lane	windmill
leaf	work
lighthouse	

words about our world

Autumn is the season between summer and winter. Many trees lose their leaves in the **autumn**.

A **calendar** tells us what day, week or month today is. Usually **calendars** begin on January 1st.

Each 100 years in history is called a **century**. We number our **centuries** from Christ's birthday. This is the 20th **century**.

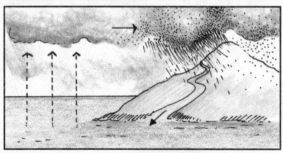

A **cloud** is millions of tiny water drops in the sky. The drops in the **clouds** fall as rain or snow.

Days have **dates** so that we can remember when things happen. The **date** of Christmas is December 25th.

A **day** lasts 24 hours. A week has 7 **days**. **Daytime** is the part of the **day** when it is light.

Earth is the name of the planet on which we live. **Earth** is also what Dad digs in the garden.

In an **earthquake**, the ground shakes or slides. **Earthquakes** kill people and destroy buildings.

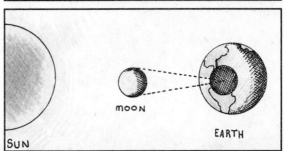

An **eclipse** happens when the sun's light cannot reach us because the moon is passing between the sun and the earth.

Evening is the time of day when the light fades. The **evening** is before the night.

An **explorer** is someone who goes where people have not been before. He **explores** unknown places.

The sea causes **floods**. Too much rain causes **floods**. Rivers overflow and **flood** the land alongside with water.

words about our world

We find **fossils** in rocks. A **fossil** is what is left of an animal or plant millions of years old.

The ground is **frozen** hard. When something **freezes** it has been made hard by the cold.

A **gale** is a very strong wind. **Gales** are dangerous for ships. **Gale** warnings are broadcast on the radio.

The **ground** is the surface of the earth. The **ground** is beneath our feet.

We measure time in **hours**. There are 24 **hours** in a day. **Hourly** means every **hour**.

A **hurricane** is a storm with a violent wind and heavy rain. **Hurricanes** are very dangerous. They destroy things and can kill people.

Ice is frozen water. When the sea is covered with **ice**, the sea is **iced** over.

An **iceberg** is a huge piece of ice that floats in the sea. Sometimes ships crash into **icebergs**.

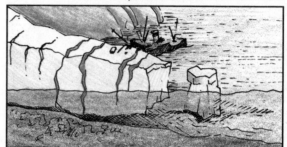

An **island** is a piece of land with water all around it. Ireland is an **island**, and so is Britain.

A **jungle** is wild land with lots of bushes, plants and trees. **Jungles** are hot and sticky.

Lightning is a flash of electricity in the sky. There is fork **lightning** and there is sheet **lightning**. It is followed by thunder.

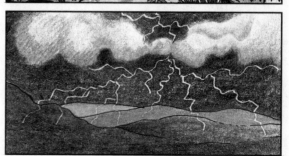

We use a **microscope** to see tiny things better. A **microscope** makes them look larger.

Midnight is the middle of the night. At **midnight** one day changes to the next.

We measure time in **minutes**. A **minute** is a short time. It lasts 60 seconds. An hour lasts 60 **minutes**.

There are 12 **months** in a year. January is the first **month**. **Months** have 30 or 31 days. The **month** of February has 28 days.

The **moon** shines at night. It goes round the earth. Sometimes we see the full **moon**. We can see all of it.

Morning is the start of the day. We get up. It gets light in the **morning**.

At **night** it is dark. We sleep. We can see the moon and the stars at **night**.

Noon is the middle of the day. It is midday. After **noon** comes the after**noon**.

A **planet** is a huge round ball that spins round the sun. Earth is a **planet**.

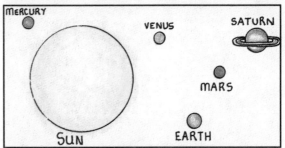

Rain is water falling from the sky. **Rain** comes from clouds. We get wet in the **rain**.

When the sun shines after rain it makes a curve of coloured light in the sky, a **rainbow**.

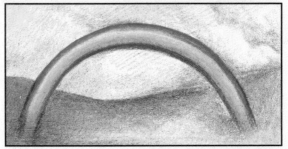

The year has four **seasons**; spring, summer, autumn, winter. **Seasonal** things happen in each **season**.

We measure time in **seconds**. A minute lasts 60 **seconds**. Some clocks tick every **second**.

On the side of you away from a light, you make, or throw, a **shadow**.

The **sky** is above the earth. Sun, clouds, moon and stars are all in the **sky**.

When a fire burns it makes **smoke**. Dad puffs **smoke** from his pipe. He is **smoking** a pipe.

Snow is white, frozen rain. **Snow** falls gently from the sky. Throwing **snowballs** is fun.

Space is what is between us and the moon and the sun and the stars.

Spring is a season. **Spring** comes after winter. Leaves begin to grow on trees in the **spring** and lambs are born.

A **star** is a round burning ball, so far away in the sky that it looks like a twinkle. The sun is the **star** nearest to earth.

A **storm** is a very strong wind. There are rain**storms**, snow**storms** and sand**storms**.

Summer is a season. It is the warmest time of the year. We have **summer** holidays.

The **sun** is a star that shines in the sky and warms everything. Without the **sun** nothing would be alive.

The **temperature** is how hot or cold something is. We use a thermometer to measure **temperature**.

When it becomes less cold, there is a **thaw**. Ice and snow melt when it **thaws**.

A **thermometer** measures our temperature. Doctor puts the **thermometer** in our mouth for a few minutes.

We hear **thunder** in a storm. It follows lightning. Sometimes there is a loud bang, or crash, of **thunder**.

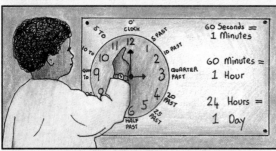

We learn about seconds, minutes and hours. We learn to tell the **time**. This all takes **time**.

Today is this day. If we are in a hurry, we must do something **today**.

Tomorrow is the next day after today. We often put off nasty jobs until **tomorrow**.

Trees are the largest plants. We need **trees**. **Trees** help to make the air good to breathe.

Volcanoes are on mountain tops. Melted rock from the earth's centre comes out of a **volcano**.

What is today's **weather**? The **weather** is good. It is sunny. It is grey, wet **weather**.

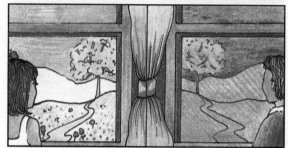

Winter is the cold season of the year. People enjoy **winter** sports, such as skiing or skating.

The sky and everything in it; the earth and everything on and in it; all this is the **world**.

We measure time in **years**. A **year** has 12 months. Each **year** begins on January 1st.

Yesterday was the day before today. We can remember **yesterday**, but **yesterday** will never come again.

These are the words you have learned in the last ten pages:

autumn	noon
calendar	planet
century	rain
cloud	rainbow
date	season
day	second
earth	shadow
earthquake	sky
eclipse	smoke
evening	snow
explorer	space
flood	spring
fossil	star
frozen	storm
gale	summer
ground	sun
hour	temperature
hurricane	thaw
ice	thermometer
iceberg	thunder
island	time
jungle	today
lightning	tomorrow
microscope	trees
midnight	volcano
minute	weather
month	winter
moon	world
morning	year
night	yesterday